FESTIVAL FOLK

An Atlas of Carnival
Customs and Costumes

ROB FLOWERS

CONTENTS

FOREWORD

By Simon Costin, Director of the Museum of British Folklore

The desire to disguise oneself is as old as humanity itself. Basically, people love dressing up! Almost every nation across the globe has some age-old ritual of becoming a character – an animal, a devil, an angel or a mythical creature. These traditional costumes are amazing, colourful and often very, very mad. So what is it about dressing up that we all love so much? Well, it's about stepping outside of our ordinary lives to become, however briefly, something extraordinary, and in doing so, to celebrate our existence.

One of the most important aspects of these celebrations is an appreciation of the power of nature, the seasons and the planet that keeps us all alive. People might choose to chase away winter in costumes of terrifying devils, and welcome in the spring with garlands of flowers and costumes of moss and straw. Moving through the year we give thanks for a plentiful harvest and the gifts of the summer season. And when the old year is over, we welcome in the new one with joyful noises and fireworks. And so, the wheel of the year turns and our seasonal traditions help us anchor ourselves within it.

These traditions also anchor us within our local communities. Each festival within the book represents the ways in which a group of people choose to express who they are and where they come from. While the costumes may all look wildly different, there are similar threads, which show that however different we may imagine we are, human beings have far more in common with each other. We all laugh, cry, sing, dance, drink and feast. And doing these things together, as a community, in a large-scale public event, helps us appreciate that shared identity, and shows the world the things that we value and find important.

Another aspect that all the festivals in this book share is an element of visual storytelling. Within these pages, you will find the legend of a 17th century Spanish woman and her miraculously cured son, giants who liberated a village from invaders, a fertility goddess released from the underworld and a magical horse who could understand human speech and was so huge three riders could sit on his back. These tales are expressed through radically creative costumes and those characters ensure that the stories are not merely repeated and dispersed, but brought to life and passed down to future generations.

Speaking of which, any naughty children reading this book better beware. There are hairy devils haunting the pages, ready to capture, whip, eat, or merely give a good telling off to anyone who has not behaved during the year! I'm sure you're not naughty though, and perhaps you've already received a gift from St Nicholas in the shape of this wondrous and beautifully illustrated book. We hope you enjoy it!

AUTHOR'S NOTE

Despite bursting into tears when my mum first put me in a Spiderman costume (I can't remember why I didn't like it, but there is definite video evidence), I've loved masks and dressing up for as long as I can remember, and for a number of years, I drove my mum mad by constantly wearing her best tea towels as capes.

Dressing up has always had a big influence on my work as an illustrator, but I reached a turning point after a trip to Romania about ten years ago, when I discovered one of my all-time favourite museums – the Museum of the Romanian Peasant in Bucharest. After learning about the incredible traditional culture and craft of that region, I managed to pick up a number of masks made of fur, dried beans, leather and cloth. This sparked an ongoing fascination with costume and ritual, which has culminated in this book.

Some of the festivals in this book have roots reaching back over a thousand years. Ancient calendars are reflected in festivals that cluster at specific times of the year: springtime, when life blooms, and harvest, when bountiful rewards are reaped from the year's labour.

This book is an introduction to some of the world's most unique and remarkable events, featuring incredible costumes, rituals and masks. Welcome to the world of Festival Folk.

ROB FLOWERS

I've wanted to create this book for a very long time and I want to acknowledge two people, without whom it would not have been possible. Amber, thank you for your support and guidance in a million small and massive ways throughout one of the toughest periods of my life. In hindsight, moving house twice, leaving London for good and teaching at four universities weren't the ideal conditions for successfully completing the most ambitious and all-consuming project I've ever undertaken. Without you, not only would it have not happened at all, but my life in general would be substantially more rubbish. I'm also very grateful to Ziggy at Cicada for being on board from the outset with the vision for this book and allowing me to do it in the way we have. It's been a labour of love, I hope you enjoy it and it leads you to find out more about these magical places, events and people.

CARNIVAL CULTURE

As you go through this book, you will find that most of the festivals happen around the same dates, particularly on or around Christian celebrations like Easter, Ash Wednesday and, particularly, Shrove Tuesday. The word 'carnival' comes from the Latin *carne levare*, meaning 'goodbye to meat', and it traditionally refers to celebrations in the month leading up to Lent, which is, in turn, a period of fasting and penitence.

From medieval times onwards, carnival involved wild street parties and parades. It provided an opportunity to turn the world upside down and celebrate the end of winter. Elaborate costumes and masks were popular, allowing commoners to hide behind them while they mocked the ruling nobility. It was a time of pranking and mischief alongside great street feasts, which used up the last of the winter stores of butter and meat before the fasting of Lent.

Some carnival customs originated in Pagan, pre-Christian traditions to do with the banishment of evil winter spirits and the welcoming of spring. These traditions were then incorporated into the Christian calendar, with Pagan wild men turning into devils, and Earth-Mother characters turning into the Virgin Mary.

Carnival is most common in Catholic countries, and many of the festivals in this book occur in the heartland of Catholic Europe and its former colonies. We have also chosen to include festival traditions outside these areas; festivals in Asia and Africa with particularly impressive costumes and traditions. These festivals share the spirit of carnival, and often celebrate harvest, the end of winter or the end of the dry season. They share a sense of hedonism and release at the end of hard times.

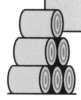

KEY DATES

EASTER

Easter is a Christian holiday celebrating the resurrection of Jesus from the dead. It usually happens sometime in March, but it is a 'moveable feast'. This means that it changes its date every year because, rather than following the solar calendar that we usually use, it is determined by a lunisolar calendar, which follows the cycles of the moon as well as the sun.

LENT

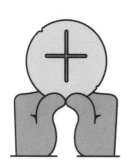

Lent is a time of repentance and fasting before Easter. It lasts 40 days.

Ash Wednesday is the first day of Lent. In some churches, the priest marks the foreheads of his congregation with an ash cross to remind them that 'from ash were you made and ash you shall be'.

SHROVE TUESDAY
(FAT TUESDAY/MARDI GRAS)

Shrove Tuesday is the day before Ash Wednesday. It is a final day of celebration and mischief before the days of penance and fasting begin. It usually occurs sometime in February. It is also a day of feasting, to use up all the fatty foods before Lent.

CORPUS CHRISTI

A Catholic festival usually held in early June to celebrate the Eucharist; the embodiment of Jesus in the holy wafer.

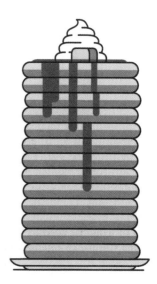

ST NICHOLAS DAY
(5TH AND 6TH DECEMBER)

In Germany and Central Europe, this day and the night that precedes it are celebrated as the time that the kindly Saint Nicholas leaves presents and his evil counterpart, Krampus, haunts the streets.

ORTHODOX CHRISTMAS
7TH JANUARY

The calendar used by Julius Caesar was known as the Julian calendar, and was replaced in 1582 by the Gregorian calendar that we use today. However, in certain parts of Eastern Europe, the Orthodox Church still uses the Julian calendar.

MAY DAY

⊙AK APPLE DAY
29TH MAY

A holiday celebrated in England to commemorate the restoration of the English monarchy.

A holiday with Pagan roots. The summer solstice was considered midsummer, and so 1st May was celebrated as the first day of summer.

PL⊙UGH M⊙NDAY

The start of the agricultural year in Britain. It is the first Monday after Epiphany (the 12 days of Christmas), which usually falls on 6th January. Plough Sunday and Plough Tuesday are also known dates.

JANUARY

FIESTA GRANDE DE ENERO
JARRAMPLAS
KUKERI FESTIVAL
MAMOIADA FESTIVAL
MALANKA
SCHNABEL PERCHTEN
VEVCANI CARNIVAL
WHITTLESEA STRAW BEAR

FEBRUARY/MARCH
(DEPENDING ON EASTER)

BUSOJARAS
CARNAVAL DE BARRANQUILLA
CARNAVAL DE BINCHE
CARNAVAL DE LAZARIM
CARNAVAL DE ORURO
CARNAVAL DE PODENCE
CARNAVAL DE VIANA DO BOLO
COURIR DE MARDI GRAS
ENTROIDO DE LAZA
KASEDORI
KASTAV BELL RINGING
NAMAHAGE
SWABIA FASTNACHT

MAY

CASTLETON GARLAND DAY
DODO CARNIVAL
OBBY OSS
PIAO SE

JUNE

EL COLACHO
HOMBRES DE MUSGO

JULY

BAJADA DE LA VIRGEN
GIANTS OF DOUAI

AUGUST

BURRYMAN
ROS BEIAARD
BOZE GOD FESTIVAL

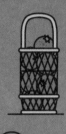

OCTOBER

PAANTU

VARIABLE DATES

THEYYAM FESTIVAL
DRAMETSE NGACHAM
DAMAS FESTIVAL
MAKISHI

DECEMBER

SILVESTERKLAUS
EL JUEGO DE LOS DIABOLITOS
KRAMPUSNACHT

FESTIVAL THEMES

Carnival traditions vary enormously from place to place. Each village has evolved distinct carnival traditions that reflect their locale and history. Costumes can be made of ribbon or rags, burlap sacks or palm leaves, and masks can be made of leather, tin or wood. However, there are some themes and traditions that are recurring, even though they are interpreted differently from place to place.

GIANTS OF DOUAI

GIANTS

Giants originated in medieval Europe and are popular traditions across France, Belgium, Spain and Germany. They measure up to nine meters high and can weight 350 kg. They are usually made of cloth over a wooden frame with head and hands made of paper mâché. Sometimes the arms and head can move around and sometimes they are fixed.

The giants usually depict respected legends from history or mythology; nobles, kings and biblical characters are common, and the stories usually relate in some way to the history of the town. As they are marched through the towns, they are followed by a parade of costumed people.

ROS BEIAARD DENDERMONDE

BIG HEADS

Where giants honour, big heads ridicule. A paper mâché head covers the wearer's head and torso, so that their limbs look comically small. They often make fun of politicians or reviled figures either from history or today. The characters usually dance and make trouble. Big heads are popular in Spain and its former colonies, and they are often paraded alongside giants.

MALANKA

KASEDORI

STRAW BEARS

Straw bears originated in the medieval carnivals of Germany, and are thought to represent Pagan 'wild men' – hairy, ogre-like men living outside civilised society in the forests. The straw bears are wrapped head to toe in straw, often with a cone-shaped headdress. They represent the banishment of winter and the welcoming in of spring and the new agricultural year.

Traditionally, the bears are led from house to house in a village, and each resident assures their fortune for the coming year by donating food, drink or money to the bear. The 'begging' aspect of the carnival was frowned upon by the Church, and in many places the festivals were banned for various periods and reinstated later.

BAJADA DE LA VIRGEN

CARNAVAL DE BARRANQUILLA

WHITTLESEA STRAW BEAR

DEVIL MASKS

Masks are an important part of carnival tradition. By hiding behind them, commoners were able to cause mischief and mock the ruling classes without fear of retribution. Devil masks are particularly important. Often made of natural materials like wood or leather, painted with terrifying features and adorned with giant animal horns, they represent both the devil and the spirit of winter, which was often chased out of the town.

NATURAL MATERIALS

Some of the festivals feature characters dressed from head to toe in natural materials like fir branches, moss, burrs or flowers. In Eastern Europe, these characters are often direct descendents of Pagan rituals banishing winter and welcoming spring. In Britain, many evolved out of Garland Day, when people would make garlands for May Day celebrations, and became so competitive with one another that characters ended up completely covered in flowers.

BURRYMAN

HOMBRES DE MUSGO

CASTLETON GARLAND DAY

ANIMAL SKINS

Animal skins feature in many festivals. They are often accompanied by masks and animal horns to create a terrifying, devil-like presence. They are usually intended to scare away the spirits of winter. They date back to times when shepherds and livestock were central to village life. They also represent the struggle between animal instinct and human reason; order and chaos.

BUSOJARAS

KASTAV

KRAMPUSNACHT

KUKERI FESTIVAL

KASTAV

KUKERI FESTIVAL

MAMOIADA FESTIVAL

COWBELLS

Bells are also very common. Like animal skins, they represent the role of the shepherd and the welcoming of spring. In some traditions such as Silvesterklausen, Mamoiada and the bell ringing of Kastav, the bells are enormous – sometimes weighing over 30 kg. The ringing of the bells is usually accompanied by the sound of drums and other traditional musical instruments. All together, they are intended to drive away the spirits of winter.

SILVESTERKLAUS

ENTROIDO DE LAZA

BONFIRES AND BURNING

A lot of festivals happen towards the end of the winter, when the days are still short and cold. Bonfires in the centre of the village are a place for people to gather and celebrate in the warmth. Another theme is the burning of reviled figures. These can take the form of a politician, the devil, or interfering village authorities. The burning of these figures is usually a moment of joy at the end of the carnival, symbolising a fresh start.

CARNAVAL DE PODENCE

NAMAHAGE

BUSOJARAS

WHITTLESEA STRAW BEAR

Forward the ritornello,
Forward the whirls,
Let's jump all together
And the heart full of songs.
    Carnival!
The most beautiful girls, the ugliest,
Young boys, old men without teeth,
You'll all have your luck
If you take advantage of the moment.
And long live Carnival!
And long live, long live Carnival!

-Traditional song of the
Carnival of Nice

BAJADA DE LA VIRGEN

LA PALMA, CANARY ISLANDS

Every five years, a statue of the Virgin of Las Nieves, patron saint of La Palma, is moved from a chapel in the mountains to the city of Santa Cruz. A big festival lasting six weeks marks this event.

Bajada means 'bringing down' in Spanish, as the statue is brought down from the mountains.

Festivities include parades of Chinese lanterns, acrobats and *Mascarones*; giant figures parading alongside people wearing big head costumes.

The centrepiece of the festival is the Dance of the Dwarves. A group of dancers wear big heads topped with enormous hats to make them look like dwarves. Despite their heavy heads, they do a fast polka dance, repeating it throughout the night until dawn.

BOZE GOD MASK FESTIVAL

AUGUST OR SEPTEMBER (VARIES)

AKUSEKIJIMA ISLAND, JAPAN

The small island of Akusekijima can only be reached via an 11-hour ferry from mainland Japan. The god of the island is called *Boze*. This festival forms part of the Bon Festival, celebrated throughout Japan.

The Bon Festival celebrates a legend in which a disciple of Buddha discovered that his mother's spirit had been taken to the realm of Hungry Ghosts. By making the correct offerings, his mother's spirit was released and he danced for joy. The festival is about honouring ancestors and it ends with a big dance.

In Akusekijima, at the end of the Bon Festival, the island men dress in terrifying Boze costumes and perform a wild dance. The costumes are made of palm husks, painted with giant, grimacing faces.

The Bozes hold a stick painted with red clay and chase small children, poking them with the stick. By frightening the children, the Bozes ensure their safety for the coming year.

BURRYMAN

SECOND FRIDAY OF AUGUST

EDINBURGH, SCOTLAND

The Burryman is dressed in a costume made entirely of prickly burrs. He parades around the Edinburgh suburb of South Queensferry from morning to night.

Around 11,000 burrs are collected from the local burdock plants and stuck together on panels, which are then wrapped around the Burryman's clothes.

He also wears a balaclava covered in burrs and a bowler hat covered in flowers.

The prickly burrs make it hard to walk, so he leans on two flower-covered sticks for support as he waddles...

He is led from pub to pub, and at each one is offered a whisky, which he must drink through a straw because of his mask. He is not allowed to speak.

BUSOJARAS

6 DAYS BEFORE ASH WEDNESDAY

MOHACS, HUNGARY

In the days leading up to Lent, around 500 men from the area around Mohacs in Southern Hungary put on terrifying masks and sheepskin cloaks and join a great parade. They wear giant cowbells that clang loudly as they march.

The parading men, called *Busos*, perform folk dances and shout at the crowd, often pulling women into a giant bear hug.

The masks are carved out of willow and coloured with animal blood. Each one is unique and should resemble the wearer.

The festival celebrates a legend in which, during the Ottoman occupation of Hungary, the people of Mohacs had to flee from the Turkish troops. They carved weapons and terrifying masks, and returned to the village at night, banging drums and yelling. The Turks believed they were demons and ran away.

The parade also features an array of other costumes as well as wildly decorated tractors, cars and horse-drawn carriages. Busos from other towns cross the Danube river in boats to join in the fun!

On the Sunday, a straw man is burned on a giant bonfire in the central square, symbolising the end of winter.

CARNAVAL DE BARRANQUILLA

4 DAYS BEFORE ASH WEDNESDAY

BARRANQUILLA, COLUMBIA

This carnival is second in size only to that of Rio de Janeiro, bringing in crowds of over a million people.

The motto of the carnival is:

THOSE WHO LIVE IT ARE THOSE WHO ENJOY IT!

The *Marimonda* is a clown, with big floppy ears and ill-fitting clothes.

He wears a mask lined with fabric tubes that creates a long, trunk-like nose.

The Dance of *Cabezones* involves people with huge heads dancing in the streets to bagpipe music.

It was inspired by similar big-head traditions from Germany.

People wearing costumes of headless men carry their heads in one hand and a machete in the other, referencing political assassinations from the 1950s.

The carnival ends with the 'burial' of *Joselito Carnival*, who symbolises the joy of the festival. People dress as either mourners or Joselito himself, to be revived at next year's carnival.

CARNAVAL DE BINCHE

3 DAYS BEFORE ASH WEDNESDAY

BINCHE, BELGIUM

The main feature of the carnival is a procession of around 1,000 clowns called *Gilles*.

This is one of many Belgian carnivals that happen in the days before Shrove Tuesday.

The Gilles wear a strange wax mask and green goggles. Nobody knows the origin of this bizarre costume.

The backs of their colourful suits are stuffed with straw to give them a hunchback.

They carry bunches of twigs, called *ramons*, and baskets full of oranges. As they walk, they throw oranges at the crowds. It is considered bad luck to throw an orange back at the Gilles, as this would be returning a gift.

They wear a belt hung with bells around their waists and wooden clogs on their feet.

On Shrove Tuesday, the Gilles parade through the streets dancing to drums. When they reach the town hall, they take off their masks.

In the afternoon, they parade again, this time wearing hats decorated with enormous white ostrich feathers.

CARNAVAL DE ORURO

SATURDAY BEFORE ASH WEDNESDAY

ORURO, BOLIVIA

The Oruro festival was originally celebrated by indigenous people in Bolivia to honour their gods. Spanish settlers allowed the festival to continue, but insisted that it be turned into a Christian celebration. The festival today blends Catholic and Native American rituals.

Oruro is a mining town, and one of the main characters of the festival is *El Tío*, a devil-like god, who is the owner of the earth's minerals. To appease El Tío, miners dance and leave him gifts of food and drink.

The parade is led by the character of *Archangel San Miguel*. Behind him is the Devil, Lucifer, surrounded by other devils, pumas, monkeys, condors and characters from Bolivian history.

Lots of different colourful costumes are on display, but the most elaborate are those of the devils, who wear terrifying carved wooden masks and embroidered suits. The Dance of the Devils is the centrepiece of the carnival.

Other characters of the festival are *Pachamama*, the Native American Earth Mother, and the Virgin Mary.

The parade ends at the local soccer stadium, and two plays are performed; one telling the story of the Spanish conquest, and the second the tale of Archangel San Miguel conquering the seven deadly sins.

After the big parade, a series of smaller parades and festivities take place, including a massive water-bomb fight, in which Westerners are the target!

CARNAVAL DE PODENCE

FAT SUNDAY & SHROVE TUESDAY

PODENCE, PORTUGAL

The main characters of this festival are the *Caretos* – men dressed as strange devils, who run around shouting and causing trouble.

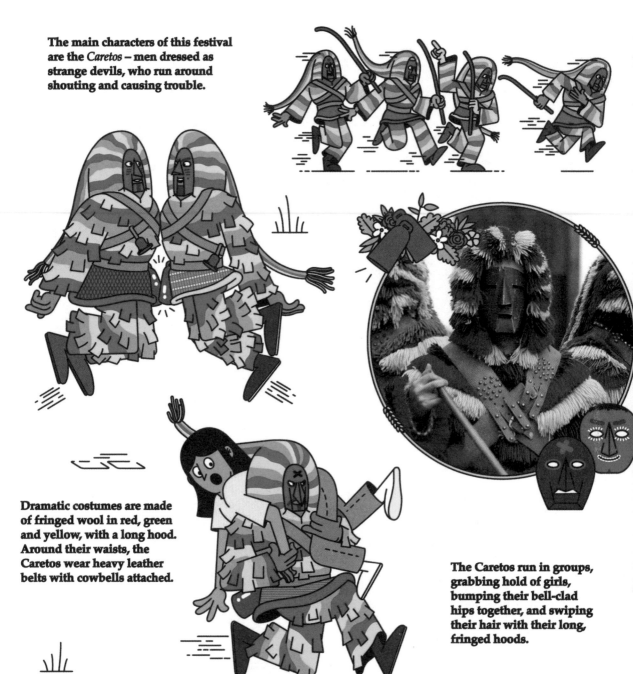

Dramatic costumes are made of fringed wool in red, green and yellow, with a long hood. Around their waists, the Caretos wear heavy leather belts with cowbells attached.

The Caretos run in groups, grabbing hold of girls, bumping their bell-clad hips together, and swiping their hair with their long, fringed hoods.

The Caretos wear red masks of leather or tin with big noses and simple devil faces painted on them.

On Fat Sunday, pretend marriages are announced between the single men and women of the village. In the morning, the 'wife' must prepare breakfast for her new 'husband'.

Unmasked men risk getting hit in the face with the Caretos' hoods.

The Caretos cause a lot of mischief – rocking cars, climbing on balconies, stealing jugs of wine, and sometimes throwing ash or other debris inside the village houses.

In the evening, a giant straw devil doll is burned in the village square.

CARNAVAL DE VIANA DO BOLO

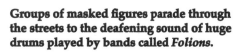
1 WEEK BEFORE ASH WEDNESDAY

VIANA DO BOLO, SPAIN

Groups of masked figures parade through the streets to the deafening sound of huge drums played by bands called *Folions*.

There are lots of different costumes, but one of the most striking is the character of *Boteiro*, who wears a grinning black mask crowned with an enormous, colourful headdress.

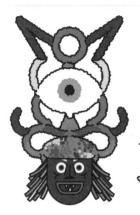

The Boteiro wears red satin trousers, leather leggings, a belt of bells and a shirt made from more than 1,000 metres of silk ribbon, sewn into geometric patterns.

Two giant dolls – the *Lardeiro* and *Lardeira* hang in the village square. Stuffed with straw and firecrackers, they are set alight at the end of the festivities.

He carries a short pole called a *monca*, and makes great leaps on it as he walks, to keep spectators away from the Folions.

Women and men of the village take turns chasing and throwing flour over each other. After the celebrations everyone sits down to feast on *androlla* – pig's stomach stuffed with pork.

CASTLETON GARLAND DAY

MAY
29

CASTLETON,
ENGLAND

A 'King' dressed in an enormous headdress of flowers rides through the village on horseback, accompanied by a Lady.

This headdress is called 'the Garland'. It is a wooden frame in a beehive shape, laden with flowers. It weighs around 25 kg and covers the entire body of the King so that only his legs are visible.

At the top of the garland is a detachable topknot made of the most beautiful garden flowers. This topknot is called 'the Queen'.

The King and the Lady are dressed in costumes of 17th century nobility.

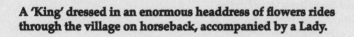

The custom dates back to Oak Apple Day, which celebrated the restoration of King Charles II to the throne in 1660.

Behind them is a procession of schoolgirls wearing white dresses and carrying 'garland sticks'. Every so often, they stop and dance a folk dance.

At the end of the parade, the Queen is removed and placed on the village war memorial. There is a big dance around the maypole.

COURIR DE MARDI GRAS

SHROVE TUESDAY

SOUTH LOUISIANA, USA

A procession of people in colourful rags travel on foot and horseback through the rural Cajun communities of South Louisiana.

Mardi Gras, or 'Fat Tuesday', is a day of feasting before Lent. Everyone knows about the big New Orleans Mardi Gras, but this lesser known event is just as fun!

A *Capitaine* on horseback herds the increasingly drunken procession from farm to farm, requesting contributions to a giant communal meal.

The tradition has its roots in medieval France. Peasants were allowed to misbehave and mock the nobility for one night of the year.

Revellers wear bright patchwork costumes and masks with beaks and pointy noses.

Their hats represent members of the medieval church and nobility of France.

The most desirable contribution is a live chicken, which is thrown off a roof for revellers to chase.

DAMAS FESTIVAL

FEBRUARY TO APRIL (VARIES)

DOGON REGION, MALI

Every few years, the Dogon people in central Mali honour dead elders with a performance called a *Dama*.

A masqueraded procession leads the souls to their final resting places.

Young men wear elaborate, traditional masks made of wood that they hold in place with their teeth. They represent members of the animal kingdom and ancestor spirits.

The *Sirige* mask is a thin, 6 m high mask carved from a single branch. It is worn by members of the village who have been present at a holy Sirige Festival, which occurs once every 60 years.

Masks vary from village to village. Some villages also perform dances on stilts.

The *Yana Gulay* mask is made of cotton and cowrie shells and represents a woman from the Fulani people.

When a boy performs in a Dama he becomes a man.

The dance lasts for three days and involves dozens of dancers. Once the Dama dance is finished, the body of the elder is placed in a sacred cave of the dead.

DODO CARNIVAL

RAMADAN · BURKINA FASO

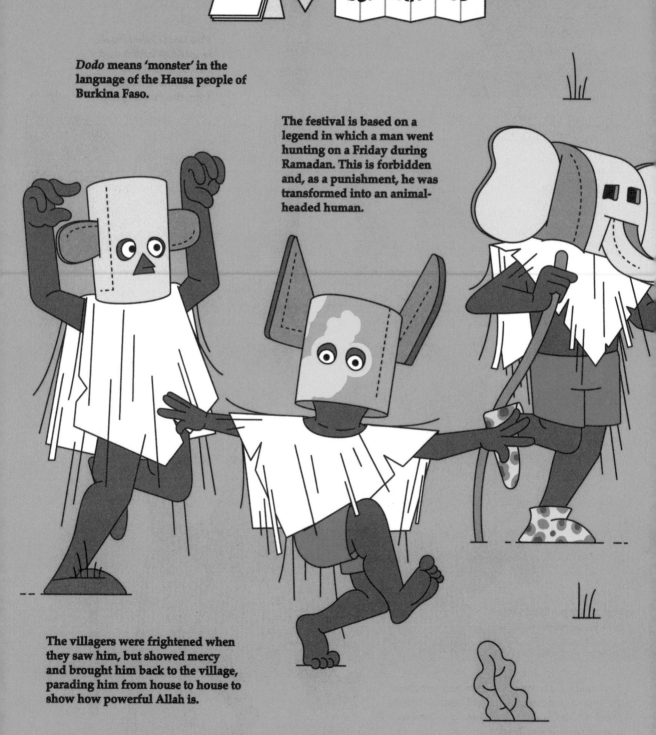

Dodo means 'monster' in the language of the Hausa people of Burkina Faso.

The festival is based on a legend in which a man went hunting on a Friday during Ramadan. This is forbidden and, as a punishment, he was transformed into an animal-headed human.

The villagers were frightened when they saw him, but showed mercy and brought him back to the village, parading him from house to house to show how powerful Allah is.

Every year at Ramadan, on a night of the full moon, a parade of people dress as Dodos in animal masks, carrying a long stick in each hand, representing paws. They go from house to house, dancing in return for gifts and money.

The Dodos dance in a repetitive rhythm to tam tam drums, making animal movements as they go.

The masks used to be made of gourds and palm stalks but are now often made of cardboard, plastic and fabric.

DRAMETSE NGACHAM

JUNE & NOVEMBER (VARIES)

DRAMETSE, BHUTAN

This festival happens twice a year at the Ogyen Tegchok Namdroel Choeling Monastery in Eastern Bhutan.

16 dancers dance to the sound of ten musicians playing on Bhutanese drums, cymbals and long horns, to honour the memory of a great Buddhist master of the 8th century, Padmasambhava.

The masks are called *uru* and they take the shape of real and mythical animals.

Before the dance starts, a clown character called 'The Old Man of Merak' warms up the crowd.

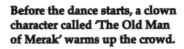

The dance lasts around three hours. It represents the circle of life and enlightenment.

The dancers wear silk jackets and loose trousers with brightly coloured silk scarves.

They hold a *chan* drum in their left hand and a curved drumstick in their right.

The dance has two parts. The first part, in the main shrine, is slow and calm to represent the peaceful gods. The second dance, outside in the courtyard, is frenzied and athletic, representing the angry gods.

EL COLACHO BABY JUMPING FESTIVAL

FEAST OF CORPUS CHRISTI — CASTRILLO DE MURCIA, SPAIN

This bizarre festival features a devil called *El Colacho*, who jumps over babies born in the previous 12 months, to cleanse them of original sin.

Wearing red and yellow suits with a masked hood, the devils run through the streets shouting at villagers and hitting them with a horsehair whip.

Babies born in the previous year are laid out on mattresses in the middle of the street. As the devils run, they leap over the babies, whilst spectators shout insults at them.

Pious men dressed in black, called *Atabaleros*, chase after the devils to the sound of drums.

The babies are then sprinkled with rose petals and returned to their parents.

The festival dates back to 1620 and is thought to have even older roots in Pagan fertility rituals.

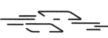

EL JUEGO DE LOS DIABOLITOS

2 DECEMBER TO 2 JANUARY

REY CURRE, COSTA RICA

This festival is celebrated by the indigenous Boruca people of Costa Rica, and it symbolises the conquest of Costa Rica by the Spanish.

A team of little devils (*Diabolitos*) tease and provoke a giant bull, who tries to 'kill' them in battles throughout the day. At last, the bull is killed and burned on the bonfire. A big party celebrates the death of the bull. The bull symbolises the Spanish forces and the devils symbolise the Boruca people.

The Diabolitos wear masks that they carve themselves out of balsa wood and a robe of banana leaves. At the end of the festival, the mask is discarded. A new one will be made the following year.

The bull wears a cedar wood mask painted in black and white, and a big burlap costume draped over a wooden frame.

FIESTA GRANDE DE ENERO

4 TO 23 JANUARY

CHIAPA DE CORZO, MEXICO

This festival celebrates a legend in which a grand, 17th century Spanish lady took her sick son to bathe in the local lake and he was miraculously cured. She hosted a great feast to express her gratitude.

At the heart of the festival is the dance of the *Parachicos*. They wear cherubic, pink carved masks. On their heads they wear helmets covered in long, yellow bristles made of a hemp-like fibre called *ixtle*, representing blonde hair.

The Parachicos also carry a metal maraca called a *chinchin*, a whistle called a *pito*, a guitar or a whip.

Other men dress as female servants. They are called *Chuntas* and they wear traditional dresses and baskets decorated with fruit and flags on their heads.

The Parachicos and the Chuntas dance to pipes and drums in a performance about relief from suffering and hunger. They hand out food and gifts as they go.

The Parachicos perform from morning till night. They stop on the way at *Priostes,* places of worship decorated with fruit and garlands.

Other highlights of the festival are a feast, a naval battle enacted in canoes and a fireworks extravaganza.

ENTROIDO DE LAZA

4 DAYS BEFORE ASH WEDNESDAY

LAZA, SPAIN

The main characters of the Laza carnival are the *Peliqueiros*.

They wear a sinister, grinning mask made of wood, topped by a large semi-circular hat that features an animal totem.

Their fur-lined jackets are worn over strange, white ruffled pants. Around their waists are cowbells.

The Peliqueiros run through the street, shouting and ringing their bells in unison. They carry a whip and hit at anyone who crosses their path.

The Peliqueiros are accompanied by a crowd of musicians making loud music to drive away evil spirits.

It is said that the costume of the Peliqueiro is that of a 16th century tax collector, who would wear a frightening costume in order to scare the townsfolk into paying their taxes.

They then go from house to house around the village. The householder has to give the Peliqueiros food and drink but is not allowed to touch them or speak their names.

The day after the Peliqueiros' parade, villagers engage in a battle, throwing flour, ash and dirt filled with live, biting ants, who have been doused in vinegar to make them extra angry!

GIANTS OF DOUAI FESTIVAL

EARLY JULY

DOUAI, FRANCE

Two giant people called *Monsieur* and *Madame Gayant* are carried through the town of Douai. They are made of wood and wicker and measure about 8 m high. It takes five men to carry each one.

The giants are moved around as they walk, inspecting their kingdom and interacting with their subjects. They are followed by townspeople wearing all sorts of costumes.

Monsieur Gayant is dressed in armour, to represent a 9th century lord who is said to have liberated the village from barbarians.

The couple is joined by their children; *Jacquot, Fillon* and *Binbin,* as well as around 100 other smaller giants of around 3 m high.

It is considered good luck to kiss baby Binbin.

The origins of the festival date to around 1530, when the city, which was then part of Spain, celebrated its defeat of the French army.

HOMBRES DE MUSGO

THE SUNDAY AFTER CORPUS CHRISTI

BEJAR, SPAIN

The *Hombres de Musgo*, or Moss Men, are six men covered from head to toe in a heavy costume of moss.

The tradition dates back to the 14th century, when a group of Christians camouflaged themselves in moss and branches and ambushed the Muslim guards at the gates of the city. The guards fled in fright and the Christians retook the city.

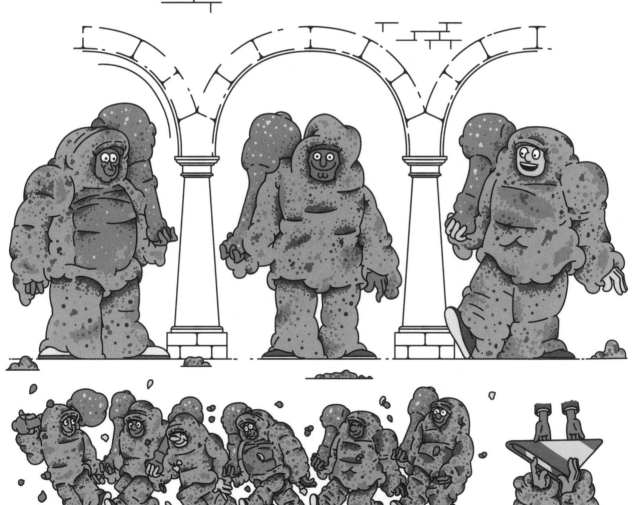

The procession marches through the old town of Bejar, along streets that are carpeted in thyme, which is believed to protect against storms. As they walk, onlookers shower the moss men with flower petals.

The procession ends up at the church in the town centre, where a flag of the old Muslim government is surrendered.

JARRAMPLAS

  JANUARY 20 — **PIORNAL, SPAIN**

The *Jarramplas* is a man dressed as the Devil, who parades through the streets, beating a drum while turnips are thrown at him.

The Jarramplas represents both the Devil and a cattle thief.

The wooden mask acts as a helmet, and he hides body armour under his colourful costume!

The hail of turnips lasts until the man gives up. It is a point of pride to last as long as possible.

By pelting the Jarramplas with turnips, the villagers are expelling the demons from their town.

22 tons of turnips are thrown each year!

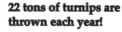

Parents in the village sign their children up at birth for a spot on the 20-year long waiting list to be a Jarramplas.

KASEDORI

FEBRUARY 11

KAMINOYAMA, JAPAN

In the Kasedori, or Straw Bird Festival, a group of men wear a cone-shaped costume made of straw called a *Kendai*.

They represent *Kase-dori*, a bird spirit who protects from fire and brings good fortune.

Kaminoyama is high in the snowy mountains of Northern Japan. The festivities start with a dance around a bonfire at Kaminoyama Castle.

KAAH!

KAAH!

KAAH!

奇習加瀬鳥

加瀬鳥

The festival is meant to bring luck to the village and prevent fires.

Girls pick strands of straw that fall off to ensure a lifetime of luxuriant hair.

The Kasedori then walk through the snow into town, calling 'kaah kaah'. Townsfolk splash them with icy water as they go.

When the festival first started in the 1600s, wooden houses were heated with open hearths, so fire prevention was very important.

53

KASTAV BELL RINGING

SUNDAY BEFORE ASH WEDNESDAY

KASTAV, CROATIA

Every Shrovetide, the men and boys of Kastav and its neighbouring towns dress in dramatic costumes to drive out the evil spirits of winter.

Called *Zvoncari*, they wear sheepskin cloaks and horned masks and carry wooden clubs. Around their waists are heavy cowbells that clang loudly.

The procession marches from village to village, covering 10-14 km.

When they get to the centre of each village, the Zvoncari stop, form a line, and swing their hips rhythmically so the bells ring in time.

The Zvoncari skip along in a zigzag motion, often colliding with each other to produce loud clanging.

The masks vary from village to village. The bell ringers of Kastav wear cattle skull masks, whilst those of Habluje wear animal masks and stripy shirts.

Pust is a puppet in the form of a reviled politician. A list of his sins is read out, and he is blamed for all the bad things that happened that year. A boat takes Pust out to sea and he is burned there.

KRAMPUSNACHT

DECEMBER 5 | GERMANY, AUSTRIA AND EASTERN EUROPE

Part goat, part demon, *Krampus* is the evil counterpart to Saint Nicholas.

Whilst Saint Nicholas gives presents to children who have been good, Krampus punishes the children who have been naughty during the year.

On Krampusnacht, men parade through the streets wearing terrifying costumes of animal skins and carved wooden masks adorned with animal horns.

NICE

NAUGHTY

They carry a bundle of birch branches, called a *ruten,* which is used to swat at passing children.

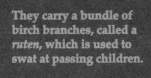

Sometimes they also carry a basket on their backs in which to cart off little children and eat them.

It is customary to offer a Krampus a shot of schnapps brandy as they pass. By the end of the night a lot of schnapps will have been drunk!

KUKERI FESTIVAL

BETWEEN NEW YEAR AND LENT

PERNIK, BULGARIA

The *Kukeri* parade through the streets of Bulgarian towns between New Year and Lent.

They scare away the evil spirits of winter with their terrifying costumes.

The costumes, which vary from region to region, usually take the shape of surreal animals or demons, with vast masks made of fur, leather, wood and ribbons.

The tradition reaches back to the Dionysian festivals of Ancient Greece when revellers would dance around in goatskins.

Big copper bells are tied around the Kukeris' waists, clanging loudly as they dance through the streets.

The biggest Kukeri festival is in Pernik at the end of January.

LAZARIM CARNAVAL

A parade of *Caretos*, or devils, march through the village, wearing enormous wooden masks, intricately carved out of tree trunks.

Despite their heavy masks, they run around the village dancing and causing trouble.

Even the children wear wooden masks.

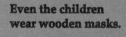

Costumes can be made from anything – rags, cane, bark, hessian or straw.

After the parade, a single man and a single woman are named the 'Godmother' and 'Godfather'. They read out embarrassing secrets of other single people in the village.

Afterwards, dolls of the Godparents are burned.

At the end, everyone eats a floury soup and a bean stew called *feijoada*, which is cooked in big pots in the middle of the street.

MAMOIADA FESTIVAL

JANUARY 17

MAMOIADA, SARDINIA, ITALY

Mamoiada is a rocky, mountainous part of Sardinia, where a big festival takes place on Saint Anthony's day.

The *Mamuthones* are the main characters of the festival. They wear dark sheep-fur vests and different black, devil-like masks with hooked noses, big foreheads and pointy chins.

On their backs, the Mamuthones carry dozens of huge cowbells, weighing over 30 kg. They are bowed down by the weight of the bells and do a strange limping dance as they walk.

To honour Saint Anthony, patron saint of animals and fire, there are over 30 bonfires throughout the village. The Mamuthones perform a special dance at each one.

Accompanying the Mamuthones are the *Issohadores*. These are cheerful bandolier-type characters with red tunics and black hats. They 'herd' the Mamuthones and engage with the crowd, lassoing women with a rope called a *soha*.

It is thought that the festival has roots in Dionysian celebrations from Ancient Greek times, banishing the winter and welcoming in the spring.

MAKISHI

EVERY 5 YEARS AT THE START OF DRY SEASON

NORTHWESTERN ZAMBIA

Every five years or so, boys of the Luvale people of Zambia undergo an initiation ritual in which they leave their childhood behind.

The ritual is called the Mukanda. It lasts between one and three months, and takes place in an isolated bush camp.

During this time the boys learn the skills they will need as a man, as well as undergoing tests of courage.

When the Mukanda is completed, a great graduation ceremony takes place, and this is called the Makishi.

Each boy is assigned a spiritual character who is represented by a special mask. These include:

Mupala; a protective spirit.

Chisaluke; a wealthy, powerful man.

Makishi; a deceased ancestor who helps the boys.

Everyone in the village comes to celebrate and the dancing goes on until morning.

Dressed in huge masks and costumes made of bark fibre, they perform a dance that they have been practicing for the past months.

At daybreak, the bush camp is set ablaze so that the secrets of the Mukanda are never revealed.

65

MALANKA

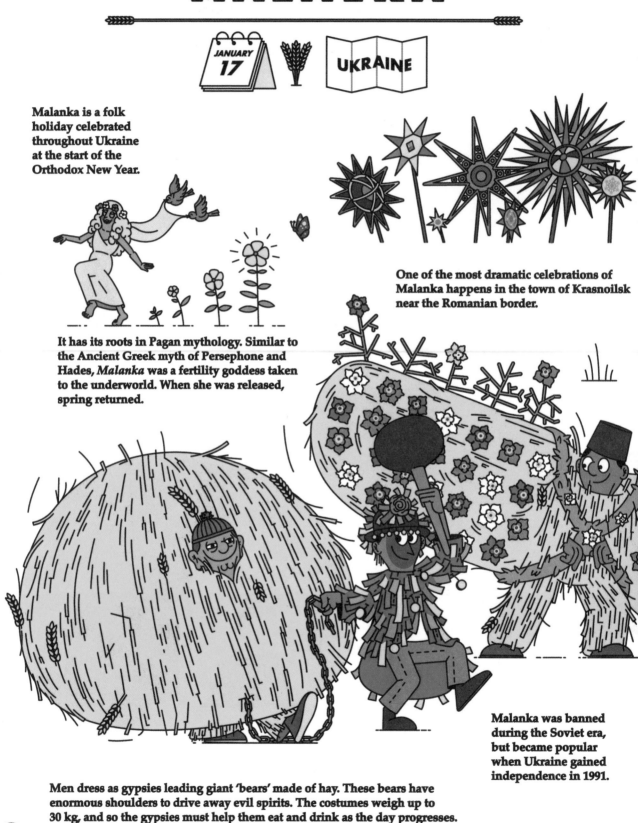

JANUARY 17 — **UKRAINE**

Malanka is a folk holiday celebrated throughout Ukraine at the start of the Orthodox New Year.

It has its roots in Pagan mythology. Similar to the Ancient Greek myth of Persephone and Hades, *Malanka* was a fertility goddess taken to the underworld. When she was released, spring returned.

One of the most dramatic celebrations of Malanka happens in the town of Krasnoilsk near the Romanian border.

Malanka was banned during the Soviet era, but became popular when Ukraine gained independence in 1991.

Men dress as gypsies leading giant 'bears' made of hay. These bears have enormous shoulders to drive away evil spirits. The costumes weigh up to 30 kg, and so the gypsies must help them eat and drink as the day progresses.

Throughout the day, they walk the streets, banging tambourines and putting on little performances.

Other people in the village dress in a random variety of costumes, some traditional and some that reference current celebrities and politicians.

As darkness falls, groups of young men put on masks and costumes and go from house to house in the towns, singing, performing funny skits and causing trouble.

In each group, one man will be the Malanka. Dressed in women's clothes, his face covered in soot and paint, he crashes around houses, spilling water and making a mess.

NAMAHAGE

OGA PENINSULA, JAPAN

During Japanese new year celebrations, local men dress in terrifying wooden masks, representing a scary ogre called the *Namahage*.

A big bonfire is built in the village square. As darkness falls, 15 Namahages come down from the mountain carrying wooden knives and buckets, grabbing at children and shouting, "are there any crybabies around?".

Afterwards, they walk through the village in pairs, knocking on doors. Wearing traditional dress, the head of the family will ask the Namahage to teach their child a specific lesson during their visit.

Once the child has been told off, the Namahage blesses the family with health and good fortune.

'OBBY 'OSS

  PADSTOW, ENGLAND

MAY 1

This is an ancient festival that has roots in the Celtic celebration of Beltane.

Two people dress up as 'Hobby Horses' (or 'Obby 'Osses) and are paraded through the town by a 'Teaser', who coaxes them along with a decorated club.

The 'Oss costume is an oval wire frame, hung with a black oilcloth cape. A scary horse mask at the front features a snapping jaw.

Following the 'Osses are two processions of local people dressed in white, dancing, playing accordions and singing.

'UNITE AND UNITE AND LET US ALL UNITE...

...FOR SUMMER IS A COME UNTO DAY...

...IN THE MERRY MORNING OF MAY.'

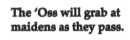

The 'Oss will grab at maidens as they pass.

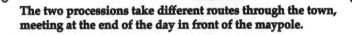
The two processions take different routes through the town, meeting at the end of the day in front of the maypole.

PAANTU

Every year, the men of the villages in Miyako-jima Island dress up as a spirit-being called *Paantu*, to expel evil spirits and bring good fortune.

Paantu wears a costume made of mud, branches and leaves. He holds a ceremonial mask made of dark wood to his face.

The Paantu men wander around the villages, smearing mud on homes, cars and people – particularly children – to ward off evil spirits.

In the past, unsuspecting tourists have got dirty and cross, and, as a result, the dates of Paantu are often not advertised widely.

PIAO SE

EARLY MAY

YAKOU, CHINA

Piao means 'floating' in Chinese. This festival is celebrated with a parade of 'floating' children.

The children wear costumes from traditional Chinese stories. The costumes hide steel bars on which the children are balanced, so they appear to float above the moving carts.

Some will even spin and do tricks as they float.

A huge, articulated wooden dragon that measures 50 m also joins the parade, performing its own special dance.

The origins are unknown. It is said that, because the area of Yakou is prone to flooding, villagers started to carry a statue of the Bodhisattva (a form of the Buddha) to protect them. The statue was eventually replaced by children.

ROS BEIAARD

LATE AUGUST | DENDERMONDE, BELGUIM

Every ten years, the town of Dendermonde comes alive with a great procession featuring a huge wooden horse.

According to medieval folksongs, *Beiaard* was a magical horse, who could understand human speech and could adjust his size to his riders. Beiaard belonged to Lord Aymon and his three brothers, who could all ride the horse simultaneously.

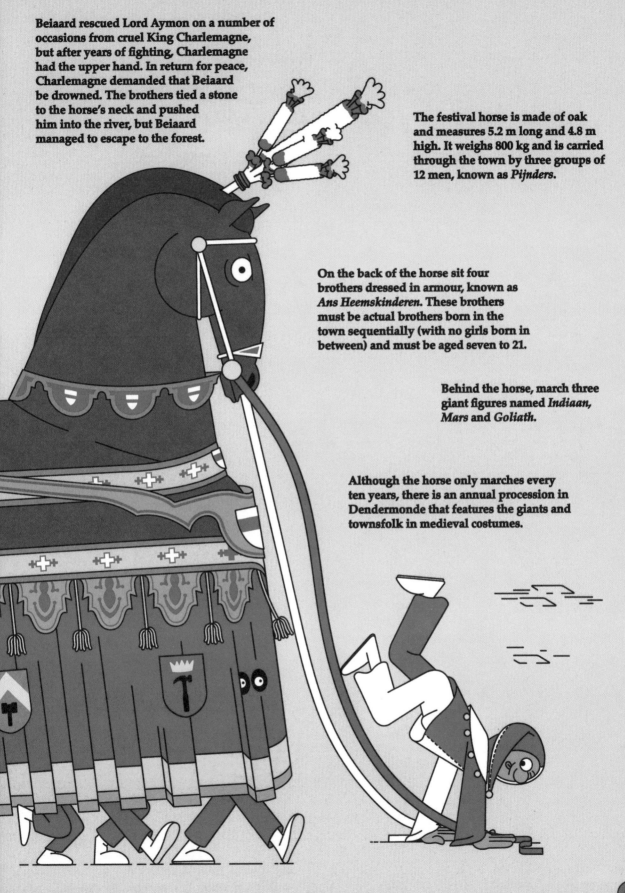

Beiaard rescued Lord Aymon on a number of occasions from cruel King Charlemagne, but after years of fighting, Charlemagne had the upper hand. In return for peace, Charlemagne demanded that Beiaard be drowned. The brothers tied a stone to the horse's neck and pushed him into the river, but Beiaard managed to escape to the forest.

The festival horse is made of oak and measures 5.2 m long and 4.8 m high. It weighs 800 kg and is carried through the town by three groups of 12 men, known as *Pijnders*.

On the back of the horse sit four brothers dressed in armour, known as *Ans Heemskinderen*. These brothers must be actual brothers born in the town sequentially (with no girls born in between) and must be aged seven to 21.

Behind the horse, march three giant figures named *Indiaan*, *Mars* and *Goliath*.

Although the horse only marches every ten years, there is an annual procession in Dendermonde that features the giants and townsfolk in medieval costumes.

SCHNABEL PERCHTEN

  JANUARY 5 ✄ **RAURIS VALLEY, AUSTRIA**

Perchta was a Pagan goddess in the Austrian Alpine region.

She appeared as an old woman with a beaked nose, wearing rags. She was in charge of making sure that holidays were celebrated correctly, houses were clean and villagers had worked hard.

There are various festivals in Austria and Germany that celebrate Perchta, but the *Schnabel Perchten* in the Alpine Rauris Valley is one of the best.

GA!
GA!
GA!

In the dark of night, on the eve of Epiphany, boys dressed in long, ragged dresses and big beaks go from house to house to make sure they have been properly cleaned.

The Schnabel Perchten carry a large pair of scissors, a needle and thread, a shovel and a broom. A basket is strapped to their backs. Their big beaks are made of linen and wood.

GA! GA! GA!

As they make their rounds of inspection, they make a strange 'ga ga ga' call. They are otherwise silent.

According to ancient legend, if your house is not clean enough, the Schnabel Perchten will slice open your stomach and fill you with all the rubbish in your house.

SILVESTERKLAUS

31 DECEMBER & 13 JANUARY

APPENZELL, SWITZERLAND

On Saint Sylvester's Day, which is celebrated twice in two weeks, groups of six people in ornate costumes go from house to house, ringing bells and singing in a very slow yodel to wish people a happy new year.

The paraders wear masks and one of three different costumes:

The 'Beautiful' costumes feature doll-like masks, giant bells and a big headdress with an intricately carved scene of Swiss peasant life. The costumes are very heavy and are only worn by men – even those costumes that feature women's clothing.

The 'Pretty Ugly' costumes are made with natural materials –
straw, moss and fir branches, woven together in careful patterns.
They are accompanied by finely woven masks and headdresses
with peasant scenes on them, all
made of natural materials.

The 'Ugly' costumes are
made of fir branches and
other natural materials,
but are much coarser
than the 'Pretty Ugly'.
The masks are terrifying
and often feature tusks
or horns.

SWABIA FASTNACHT

FAT THURSDAY TO ASH WEDNESDAY

SWABIA, GERMANY

Fastnacht, or Fasching is a carnival celebrated in Germany, Austria and Switzerland.

The costumes of Swabia in Southwest Germany are particularly interesting. They take the shape of animals, witches, demons and jesters called *Narren*.

NARRO!

Throughout the week leading up to Ash Wednesday, a string of processions march through the towns of Swabia.

One of the most famous Narren is *Federahannes* – a mischievous clown known for stealing hats, who wears a coat decorated with white feathers.

The jesters make lots of noise to scare away the spirits of winter, calling 'narro narro' as they walk along.

NARRO!

Lange Man is a giant on stilts. *Geisenmeckerer* is a devil with horns and a goatee.

NARRO!

Gschell is a friendly character with bells strapped to his chest.

The masks are usually carved from wood, and are influenced by the masks of Commedia dell'arte in Italy.

NARRO!

The festival originated in medieval times, and allowed peasants to mock the ruling aristocrats from behind their costumes.

During Fastnacht, it is traditional to eat *schmotzig*, which means lard or grease, and usually comes in the form of donuts.

THEYYAM FESTIVAL

DECEMBER TO APRIL (VARIES)

NORTH MALABAR, INDIA

Known as the 'dance of the gods', Theyyam is a Hindu ritual celebrated in the Kerala area.

The Theyyam is performed by lower caste people, traditionally untouchables, who, for one night, are transformed into oracles!

They perform a dance in front of the village shrine. The first part of the dance is done in normal clothes and the second part is performed in a magnificent costume.

Painted in reds and oranges, the dancer wears an enormous headdress made of bamboo, feathers, coconut leaves and flowers. It reaches 3 m high and weighs around 50 kg! Sometimes someone needs to support the headdress from behind.

VEVCANI CARNIVAL

13 & 14 JANUARY

VEVCANI, MACEDONIA

Every year, the village of Vevcani has a riotous festival held on Saint Vasilij's day – the beginning of the New Year according to the Julian calendar.

With roots in Pagan traditions, the festival allows villagers to 'turn the world upside down' for one night.

Revellers wear masks and costumes that mock celebrities, politicians and current events of the previous year. The streets are filled with satirical street theatre.

A great parade runs through the town. Traditional music is played on drums and a woodwind instrument called a *zurla*, with others banging on pots, pans, bells and anything else they can get their hands on.

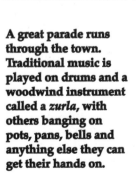

After the parade, the riotous festivities continue through the night.

WHITTLESEA STRAW BEAR

PLOUGH TUESDAY

WHITTLESEA, ENGLAND

Straw bears are a popular carnival tradition in Germany. They are also are the highlight of a festival in this small town in the East of England.

A man or boy has long lengths of straw wrapped around his arms, legs and body. His head is completely covered by a giant straw cone.

A procession accompanies the bear, featuring Morris dancers, longsword and clog dancers and a decorated plough.

A 'Keeper' leads him from house to house, dancing in return for food, beer or money.

The tradition has roots in medieval times, but it fell out of favour in the early 20th century. It was revived in 1980.

The festivities end with a 'Bear Burning'. A new costume will be made for next year's festival.

EUROPE

BURRYMAN

CASTLETON GARLAND DAY

WHITTLESEA STRAW BEAR

SWABIA FASTNACHT

OBBY OSS

ROS BEIAARD DENDERMONDE

GIANTS OF DOUAI

CARNAVAL DE BINCHE

SILVESTERKLAUS

CARNAVAL DE VIANA DO BOLO

ENTROIDO DE LAZA

EL COLACHO

CARNAVAL DE PODENCE

LAZARIM CARNIVAL

HOMBRES DE MUSGO

JARRAMPLAS

MAMOIADA FESTIVAL

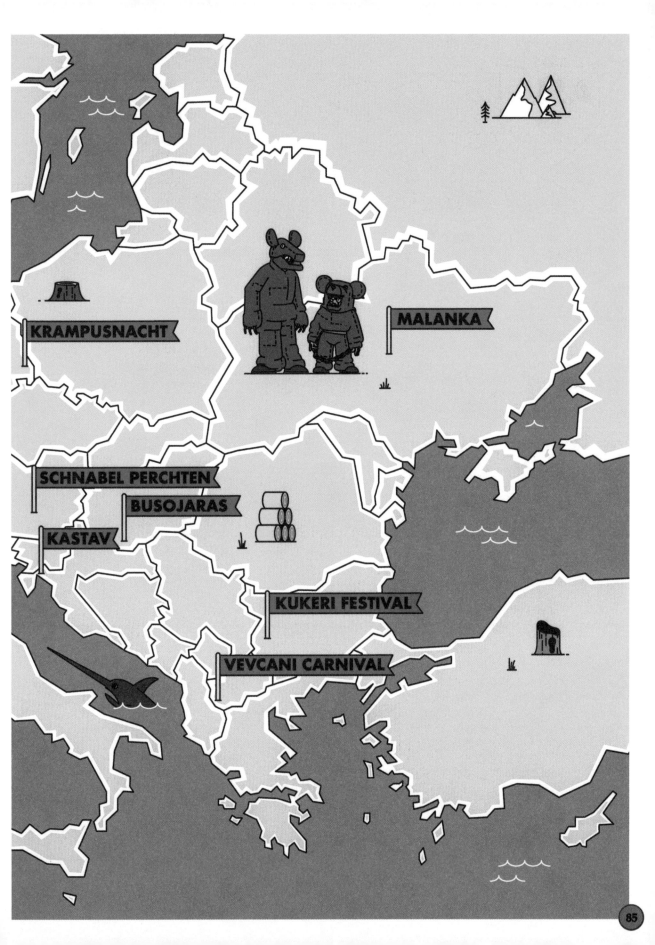

KRAMPUSNACHT

MALANKA

SCHNABEL PERCHTEN

BUSOJARAS

KASTAV

KUKERI FESTIVAL

VEVCANI CARNIVAL

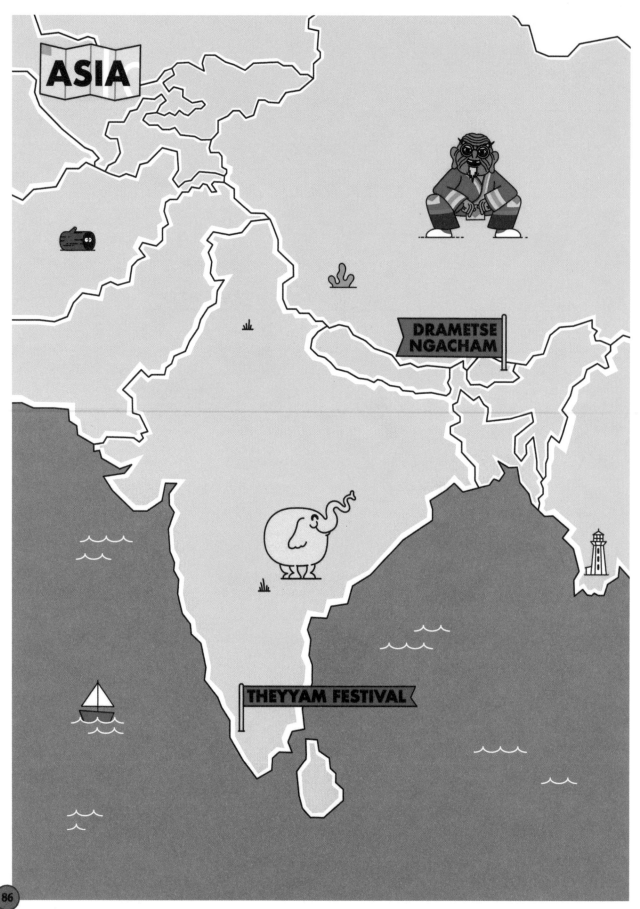

ASIA

DRAMETSE
NGACHAM

THEYYAM FESTIVAL

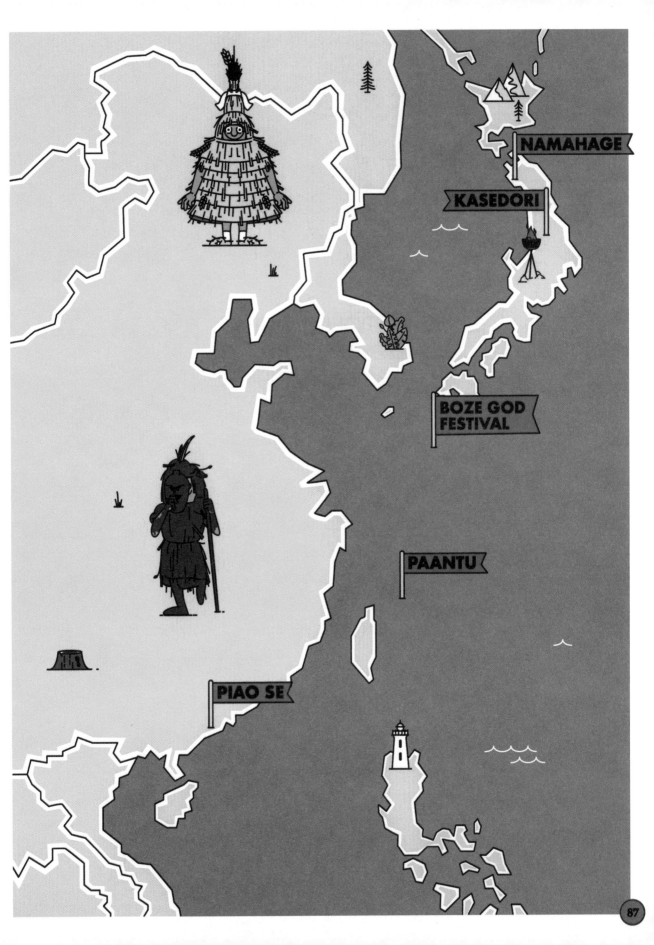

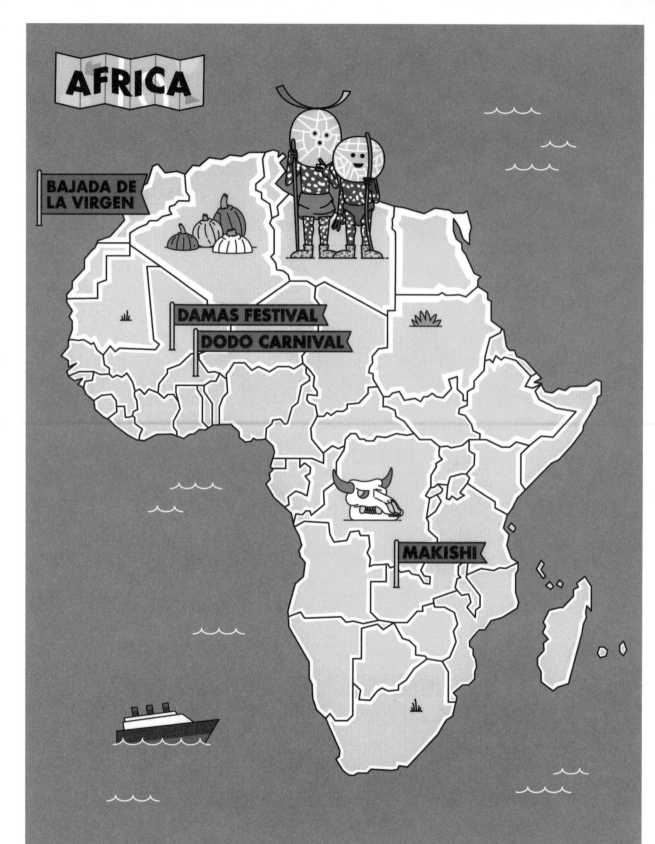

AFRICA

BAJADA DE
LA VIRGEN

DAMAS FESTIVAL

DODO CARNIVAL

MAKISHI

COURIR DE
MARDI GRAS

FIESTA GRANDE
DE ENERO

EL JUEGO DE
LOS DIABOLITOS

CARNAVAL DE
BARRANQUILLA

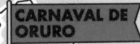

CARNAVAL DE
ORURO

FURTHER FESTIVAL FUN

There are countless other weird and wonderful festivals all over the world. Organised by country, this is a small selection that feature particularly spectacular traditions and costumes.

BAHAMAS
JUNKANOO

SAO NICOLAU, CAPE VERDE
CAPE VERDE CARNIVAL

DOMINICIAN REPUBLIC
DOMINICIAN REPUBLIC CARNIVAL

GUARANDA, ECUADOR
GUARANDA CARNIVAL

WHITSTABLE & HASTINGS, ENGLAND
JACK IN THE GREEN

PRATS-DE-MOLLO-LA-PRESTE, FRANCE
FESTIVAL OF THE BEARS

FRENCH GUIANA
FRENCH GUIANA CARNIVAL

NAOUSSA, GREECE
NAOUSSA CARNIVAL

KISSLEGG, GERMANY
KISSLEGG CARNIVAL

SACHSENHEIM, GERMANY
URZELNZUNFT

OTTANA, SARDINIA, ITALY
OTTANA CARNIVAL

SKYROS, GREECE
NAOUSSA CARNIVAL

OROTELLI, SARDINIA, ITALY
OROTELLI CARNIVAL

DRAMA, MACEDONIA
ARIPIDES FESTIVAL

SAPPADA, ITALY
SAPPADA CARNIVAL

URUS, MOLDAVIA
URUS BEAR FESTIVAL

DOBRA, POLAND
ŚMIGUS-DYNGUS

TRAMIN, ITALY
TRAMIN FASNACHT

PTUJ, SLOVENIA
KURENTOVANJE

JAPAN
LONG, RED NOSED
GOBLIN FESTIVAL

PODGRAD, SLOVENIA
SKOROMAT FESTIVAL

AVILA, SPAIN
FESTIVAL NAVALOSA

MECERREYES, SPAIN
MECERREYES CARNIVAL

GUADALAJARA, SPAIN
DEVIL CARNIVAL OF LUZON

VALDESOTO, SPAIN
SIDROS Y COMEDIES

ALSASUA, SPAIN
CARNAVAL DE ALSASUA

SILIO, SPAIN
LA VIJANERA FESTIVAL

VAL DE HERENCE, SWITZERLAND
CARNIVAL EVOLENE

LOTSCHENTAL, SWITZERLAND
TSCHAGGATTA

TRINIDAD
TRINIDAD CARNIVAL

INDEX

Festival Folk
Published by Cicada Books Limited
Illustrated by Rob Flowers
Written by Ziggy Hanaor and Rob Flowers
British Library Cataloguing-in-Publication Data. A CIP
record for this book is available from the British Library.
ISBN: 978-1-908714-57-2

Rob Flowers is an illustrator with a distinctively bold
style, defined by crayon-bright palettes, playful forms
and eccentric characters. He is a keen collector of kitsch
ephemera and historical miscellany including 80s gross
out toys, 70s cartoons and early McDonalds advertising
memorabilia. His clients include: The British Museum,
The Museum of Witchcraft & Magic, Children in Need,
Action Aid, The Museum of Childhood, The Natural
History Museum and The Museum of Briitish Folklore.

Festival Folk is his first book.